The Budding Gardener

Edited by Mary B. Rein
Illustrations by Jane Dippold

Acknowledgments

The following individuals contributed ideas and activities to this book:
Anne Adeney, Linda Atamian, Laura Claire-Gremett, Sharon Dempsey, Laura Durbrow, Sue Bradford Edwards, Kay Flowers, Karen Gassett , Virginia Jean Herrod, Erin Huffstetler, Mary Ann Kohl, Barb Lindsay, Eileen Lucas, Jayne Morrison, Sandra Nagel, Shirley Anne Ramaley, Dani Rosensteel, Kim St. George, Barbara Saul, Debbie Vilardi, Jackie Wright

THE *Budding* GARDENER

EDITED BY MARY B. REIN

©2011 Gryphon House, Inc.

Published by Gryphon House, Inc.
10770 Columbia Pike, Silver Spring, MD 20901
301.595.9500; 301.595.0051 (fax); 800.638.0928 (toll-free)

Visit us on the web at www.gryphonhouse.com

Cover photograph courtesy of iStock Photography

Library of Congress Cataloging-in-Publication Data
The budding gardener / edited by Mary B. Rein.
    p. cm.
 ISBN 978-0-87659-373-8
1. Gardening—Juvenile literature. I. Rein, Mary B.
 SB457.B73 2011
 635—dc22
                              2010045539

Bulk Purchase
Gryphon House books are available for special premiums and sales promotions as
well as for fund-raising use. Special editions or book excerpts also can be created to
specifications. For details, contact the Director of Marketing at Gryphon House.

Disclaimer
Gryphon House, Inc. cannot be held responsible for damage, mishap, or injury
incurred during the use of or because of activities in this book. Appropriate and
reasonable caution and adult supervision of children involved in activities and
corresponding to the age and capability of each child involved, is recommended at
all times. Do not leave children unattended at any time. Observe safety and caution
at all times.

Contents

Contents

Chapter Four: Taking Care of Your Garden

Chapter Five: Just for Fun

Introduction

How to Get Started

Gardening with your child can be as small and simple as sprinkling grass seed on a damp sponge, or as large and complicated as growing a vegetable garden that will feed the neighborhood. No matter where or how you begin, gardening cultivates observation, patience, and responsibility, and offers rewards beyond measure.

This is a book of ideas. Page through it and start with something that appeals to you and to your child. Let one thing lead to another. Follow your child's lead and your own interests, and you cannot go wrong.

Happy gardening!

Chapter 1
Watch It Grow

Let's Make a Garden!

Here is a simple, child-friendly garden. You can add to it and make it your own as you and your child discover what you enjoy doing together. Refer back to this page whenever you need a refresher.

What You'll Need

rake (use a child-sized rake if you have one)

seeds or seedlings (herb, flower, or vegetable)

shovel

sunny, outdoor garden area

topsoil or compost (see page 48)

trowel

watering can

What to Do

1. Choose a sunny spot. Start small, maybe 3' by 3'—you can always enlarge the garden later.

2. Your child can help you prepare the soil. With the shovel, dig up the planting area to loosen the soil. You should do the heavy digging and encourage him to break up the clumps of dirt with his hands and the trowel.

3. Add a good layer of topsoil or compost (you can buy a bag at the garden center). You dig it in, then your child can help you rake the area smooth.

4. Demonstrate how to plant a seed by digging a small hole with the trowel, putting a couple of seeds in it, and covering them with soil. If you are using seedlings, show how to dig a small hole, insert the seedling, and press soil gently around it.

5. Water everything well.

6. Check the garden every day and water when needed. (See "Taking Care of your Garden" on pages 46–58, for ideas about weeding and pest control.)

7. As the plants grow, enjoy the changes with your child.

8. As they become ready, pick flowers and herbs for the house and vegetables for the kitchen.

9. You may want to keep a simple journal with your child, recording in words and pictures how the garden grows.

Growing Three Sisters

This is a gardening activity and a way to learn about the cultures that Europeans found when they arrived in the Americas. For thousands of years, people all over the world have been gardening, and we can learn from them all.

What You'll Need

a sunny area at least 4' by 4'

compost (see page 48)

corn, pole beans, and squash seeds (you can use zucchini or winter squash, or both)

shovel

soil

trowel

Books to Share

Corn Is Maize by Aliki

One Bean by Anne Rockwell

What to Do

1 Talk with your child about Native American cultures and pay a visit to the library. The Iroquois nations and many other tribes called corn, beans, and squash "The Three Sisters." Native Americans planted these vegetables together, and the three plants helped each other just as human brothers and sisters do. Corn grows tall and gives the beans something to climb on. Beans add nitrogen to the soil to fertilize the corn and the squash. Bristly squash stems keep animals from eating the other plants.

2 If you are going to plant in an area that has not been planted before, use the shovel to remove the grass or sod, and loosen the soil to prepare a garden bed.

3 Mark four rows of four holes each. You and your child can work together to dig each hole 4" to 6" deep. Space the holes about 1' apart.

4 Mix compost (see page 48) with the soil you have removed from the holes. This is a great job for your child, using hands or a trowel.

5 Help your child overfill the holes with the compost and soil mixture. Don't stop until you have a small mound (4" high and 12" wide) on top of each hole.

6 Plant four corn seeds in each mound, making a small circle around the center of the mound. Water these seeds well.

7 Check them every day and keep them watered. When the corn is 4 to 6" tall, plant four bean seeds, one on each side of the mound and about half way down the mound, and plant four squash seeds around the base of each mound.

8 As the beans grow, wind them around the corn stalks.

Start Squash Indoors

Squash is a great plant for children. It grows quickly and produces impressive vines and an abundant harvest. Start it indoors to make it even more interesting.

What You'll Need

large tray or newspaper to protect the work surface

old spoon

paper cups (poke a hole in the bottom of each, for drainage)

potting soil

squash seeds

water and sunlight

What to Do

1. Place materials on a large tray or on a table covered with newspaper.
2. Have your child scoop soil into each cup.
3. Put a seed on top of the soil and cover lightly with more soil.
4. Water well.
5. Place the plants in sunlight.
6. Wait and watch, checking every day and watering as needed.
7. When the seedlings are strong and sturdy, plant them outdoors in your garden and watch them grow!

Use What You Have

You already have simple containers for starting seeds! You or your child may come up with more ideas of your own.

What You'll Need

an old plastic ice cube tray or a clean egg carton

seeds of your choice

sunny windowsill

water

What to Do

Your child can do all of these steps, with supervision.

1. Poke a small hole in the bottom of each cup of your ice cube tray or egg carton so that the water can drain.
2. Fill each cup with potting soil.
3. Plant two or three seeds in each cup.
4. Water, and place on a sunny windowsill.
5. Check daily, and keep the soil moist.
6. Once the seeds have sprouted, pinch off the smallest plants so that you have one strong plant per cup.
7. When the seedlings are sturdy, plant them outside in your garden.

Make a Mini-Greenhouse

You and your child can start plants indoors in the early spring, and they will be ready to plant outdoors when the soil warms up. Or, if you plant lettuce, spinach, or beet seeds in a mini greenhouse, you can use the tiny leaves and greens any time as a delicious addition to your salad.

What You'll Need

a small watering can

clear plastic berry boxes with hinged lids

potting soil (you can buy a bag at the hardware store or garden center)

seeds of your choice

What to Do

Your child can do all of these steps, with supervision.

1. Rinse out the berry boxes.
2. Fill them about half full of potting soil and plant the seeds inside. Try fast-growing plants such as beans, lettuce, radishes, and thyme to keep your child captivated throughout the growing process.
3. Water lightly, then close the lid.
4. Place the finished greenhouses in a sunny location. Put something under them to catch drips. Keep the lids closed on cold days; open them on warm days.
5. Water as needed, but don't let the soil get soggy. Explain that the "greenhouse effect" keeps moisture in.
6. When the seedlings are ready and all danger of frost is past, help your child transfer them to the garden.

A Greenhouse in My House

Here is another simple way to have a greenhouse indoors. This one will accommodate larger plants.

What You'll Need

clear plastic bags big enough to cover each plant without impeding growth

seedlings in pots

sticks to support the tops of bags (12" to 18" tall)

What to Do

1. Talk about greenhouses and how they help plants grow by holding in moisture and warmth. If there is a real greenhouse nearby at a plant nursery or in a city park, you might want to plan a visit.

2. To make this very simple indoor greenhouse, first water the seedlings in the pots well, and let them drain. Then insert two or three sticks into each pot, and put the pot inside a clear plastic bag so the sticks hold the plastic away from the plant. Blow into the bag to puff it up, and tie it closed.

3. If you want, leave a few plants uncovered for comparison.

4. As the days go by, guide your child to notice the condensation inside the greenhouses. You can discuss the water cycle. Do the plants in the greenhouses grow faster than the ones you left uncovered? Do they need watering less often?

5. Before you remove the bags, have your child slip a finger or two inside to feel the moisture. Smell the air inside the greenhouse. Remove the greenhouses when the plants get crowded, and transfer the plants outdoors.

My Greenhouse

Fall Planting

This is an exercise in patient waiting, with a joyful surprise at the end. The bulbs sprout and bloom in the spring when we have almost forgotten about them!

What You'll Need

bulbs: snowdrop, crocus, daffodil, tulip

bulb food (from the garden center)

shovel

topsoil

trowels

watering can

What to Do

1. Identify the outdoor area you want to use as a garden bed. Prepare it for planting by turning over the dirt (see page 10).
2. Add topsoil and bulb food, if needed.
3. You and your child can work together to dig holes for the bulbs. You will need one hole per bulb, and the holes need to be about twice as deep as the size of the bulb.
4. Put the bulbs in the holes, rounded side down, and press firmly.
5. Refill the holes with dirt.
6. Water well and wait until spring!

Another Thought

You do not have to create one flower bed. You can plant bulbs individually wherever you want them for an extra surprise when spring comes.

Watch Them Sprout

This project has several simple components: collecting the seeds, setting things up, and watching the seeds sprout. It offers an opportunity to watch the growth that usually happens underground, invisible to us.

What You'll Need

an assortment of seeds (see "What to Do" for ideas)

a small amount of purchased grass seed (optional)

clear plastic cups

paper towels

permanent marker, or paper to make labels

plastic wrap

shallow dish

sponge

What to Do

1. Collecting the seeds you and your child want to observe is part of the fun. You might include grass seed, seeds collected from fruit in your kitchen (for example: apples, grapefruit), dried beans (lentils work especially well), or seeds collected outdoors. Try any seed that interests you. Some will sprout, and some will not. Some will be quick and some will be slow. This project can be as large or as small as you and your child wish!

2. As you collect the seeds, put them in envelopes or small plastic bags and label them, or note where you found them. This will add interest to the project.

3. If you are using grass seed, wet the sponge and have your child sprinkle grass seeds all over it. Put the sponge in the shallow dish and add water so it stays damp. Children, especially young ones, enjoy watching grass sprout and grow on the sponge. You can do this over and over again! Just pull off the grass, wash the sponge, and it is ready for the next time.

4. For all other seeds, have your child wet a paper towel and fold it to fit inside a clear plastic cup or a small zip-top bag. Help her slip a few seeds between the paper towel and the clear plastic so they are easily visible. Add a tablespoon or two of water for the towel to absorb.

5. Do this for as many seeds as you want. Label them, cover the cups with plastic wrap, and put them in a dim spot until they start to sprout. Be sure the towels stay damp.

6. Once the seeds have sprouted, move them into the light so you can watch the leaves turn green.

7. At this point, you can decide if you want to continue by planting your little plants in pots.

Grow... Grow... Grow!

Fishbowl Jungle

Here is another way to watch seeds sprout. This one is pure fun—your child may want to use the fishbowl jungle "habitat" for play with small toy jungle animals. You can talk about jungles and rainforests if you want.

What You'll Need

clear plastic wrap

cotton balls

fish bowl

garden pea seeds

water

What to Do

1. Arrange a layer of cotton balls in the bottom of the fish bowl.
2. Wet the cotton thoroughly; all water should be absorbed by the cotton, so pour out any excess water.
3. Sprinkle the seeds over the cotton.
4. Cover the bowl with plastic wrap and place it near a window.
5. Watch it each day and keep it moist. The seeds will sprout, and eventually the vines will completely fill the bowl, creating a miniature jungle.

18

Plants from the Kitchen

Watch familiar vegetables turn into sturdy plants right on your windowsill.

What You'll Need

fresh carrots

shallow dish or saucer

sweet potato

tall glass or jar large enough to hold the sweet potato

toothpicks

water

What to Do

For the carrot:

1. Slice about ½" from the top of the carrot (the thick end).
2. Put the slice of carrot into the dish or saucer with the cut side down, and put enough water in the dish to reach halfway up the carrot slice.
3. Put the saucer in a sunny window, and replenish the water as needed.
4. After a few days you will see that the carrot greens are growing.

For the sweet potato:

1. Cut about ½" off the thicker end of the sweet potato.
2. Halfway up from the cut, push several toothpicks into the sweet potato to support it in the glass.
3. Suspend the sweet potato in the glass, and fill it up with water so the bottom of the vegetable is completely submerged.
4. Wait and watch. Add water as needed to keep the level constant. Be patient: It will take anywhere from 10 days to two weeks for the potato to begin to sprout.
5. Once the roots are well-developed, the sweet potato can be planted in a pot and will make a beautiful houseplant.

19

Saving Seeds

Our forefathers and foremothers did it, but saving seeds is something we rarely consider today. It is very satisfying and very simple.

What You'll Need

cookie sheets or trays for drying seeds

envelopes

markers

Books to Share

Seeds by Ken Robbins

The Story of Johnny Appleseed by Aliki

What Kind of Seeds are These? by Heidi Bee Roemer

Thinking ahead

Include several plants in your garden with easy-to-harvest seeds. Cosmos, marigolds, sunflowers, impatiens, morning glory, cleomes, zinnia, sweet peas, and coriander are all good choices.

What to Do

1. Observe the plants throughout the growing season.
2. Talk about reasons to save seeds: to preserve history, to save money, to share with others. (See "Memory Garden," on page 38.)
3. When the seeds are ready to harvest, show your child how to collect them. Then step back, and let him do the work. If you are unsure how to harvest the seeds from a particular plant, look online for instructions. (Search for "saving garden seeds," or try this website: www.kidsgardening.com/growingideas/projects/aug04/pg1.html.)
4. Spread the collected seeds out on a cookie sheet or tray, and allow them to dry for at least a week (a cool spot indoors is best).
5. Your child can decorate envelopes for saving the seeds. Encourage him to draw a picture of the plant, label it, and write or dictate simple growing instructions based on what you observed in your garden. This is especially nice if you will be using them for gifts.
6. Place the seeds in the envelopes.
7. Store them in a cool, dry location until next spring.

Chapter 2
Gardening Indoors and in Containers

Spring in the Middle of Winter

This is a classic indoor growing experience. It will fill your home with beauty and fragrance in the coldest, darkest months of the year.

What You'll Need

a shallow bowl which will hold several bulbs, or individual cups large enough to hold one bulb each

paper-white narcissus bulbs (available at hardware stores and garden centers in the fall)

small stones or marbles (the natural gravel sold for fish tanks is ideal)

water

What to Do

Your child can carry out every part of this activity.

1. Fill the bowl or cups with stones or marbles to about ½" of the top.

2. Use your hands to make a shallow depression in the stones for each bulb you want to plant. They can be very close together.

3. Set the bulbs in the depressions, root side down, and mound the gravel up around them a little to hold them steady. The top half of each bulb should remain uncovered.

4. Add water to cover the stones and the bottom of the bulbs.

5. Place the containers in a well-lighted place.

6. Add water every day, as needed, to keep the bottom of the bulbs submerged. Wait and watch. In a week or two, you will see green sprouts, and shortly afterwards, buds will appear, then fragrant flowers.

Amaryllis

Here is another spring-in-winter experience. Because amaryllis plants grow so dramatically tall and have such large flowers, it can be fun to measure and record their growth.

What You'll Need

a piece of poster board or other large paper

amaryllis bulb in a pot

camera (optional)

markers

ruler

water

yardstick

What to Do

① In December, you can find amaryllis bulbs in pots for sale at most hardware and home supply stores and in many supermarkets. These fast-growing bulbs grow to about 2' tall and have huge bright blooms.

② Put the potted bulb on a saucer to catch the drips, and water it well, following the instructions on the box it came in. Put it in a bright spot.

③ Find a place to hang up the paper. When the green shoots appear, have your child use the ruler to measure them every day and to draw a line on the paper to record their height. It is an exciting day when the flower bud shows itself! Finally, when the ruler is not long enough, start using the yardstick.

④ When the blooms open, you may want to measure them, too.

⑤ Each day, if necessary, remind your child to be the gardener who will check to see if the plant needs water, add water if needed, and then do the measuring.

⑥ You may want to take pictures to document this remarkable plant.

23

An Indoor Herb Garden

An indoor herb garden offers a multisensory gardening experience at your fingertips. Textures, smells, and flavors, all on your kitchen windowsill.

What You'll Need

newspaper to cover the work surface or an old plastic tablecloth

old spoon to use as a small trowel

potting soil

small herb plants

small pots

watering can

What to Do

1. Take your child to visit a local nursery, and talk with an employee about which herbs do well indoors. Be sure your child is included in the conversation, and be sure he helps pick out the herbs for his indoor garden. Three or four herbs will be enough for a young child to start.

2. Discuss potting soil with the employee and what size pots to use.

3. Back home, choose a windowsill or other appropriate place for the herbs. It should have plenty of light. It is especially nice if it can be in the kitchen.

4. Cover your work surface with the newspaper or plastic tablecloth.

5. Working with your child, show him how to pot the first herb, using his hands, the spoon, and the potting soil. When it is settled in the pot, water it well. Let him do the rest on his own, but stay nearby in case he needs help.

6. Set the pots on the windowsill and remind him to water as needed.

7. When the herb plants are big enough, show your child how to cut off just enough to use for cooking. If he helps cook with his own herbs, you may soon have a budding chef as well as a gardener!

Mini-Terrarium

It is fun to create a small habitat in a container. If you choose tropical plants, partially cover the opening of the fish bowl with plastic wrap to increase the amount of humidity inside.

What You'll Need

a clear glass or plastic container with a wide opening (a goldfish bowl or a small fish tank is ideal)

a few small plants (Visit a garden center and look for small houseplants. Ivy and asparagus ferns are hardy and usually do well. For flowers, you might choose violas, small petunias, or miniature African violets.)

colorful aquarium rocks or other small gravel

newspapers or an old plastic tablecloth to cover your work area

plastic measuring cup or other cup, for scooping dirt

potting soil

What to Do

1. Spread old newspaper or an old plastic tablecloth over your work area.
2. Set out the container. Your child should fill it about ¼ full with colorful rocks or gravel.
3. Now, using the cup, he can scoop potting soil into the container, filling it to about the halfway mark.
4. Demonstrate how to remove the plants from their plastic nursery pots.
5. With his small hands, let him make holes in the dirt and plant the little plants in the fish bowl. Press the dirt firmly around the roots and add a little more dirt if needed to keep them in place.
6. Water the terrarium.
7. For clean-up, bundle the excess potting soil in the old newspaper or tablecloth and take it outside.
8. Place the indoor mini-garden near a sunny window but not in direct sun, and water it about twice a week. Do not overwater this enclosed space! Your child may need guidance, but he will enjoy the responsibility of watering.

Succulent Garden

Succulents are terrific indoor plants that require very little maintenance and grow slowly. They have unusual shapes and growth habits, and you will discover very soon that they can be propagated easily from cuttings or from the leaves that break off accidentally.

What You'll Need

a curved piece of plastic cut from a deli container

a few succulent plants (see "What to Do" for ideas)

a wide pot with good drainage

clean sand

rocks or pebbles

soil mixed with sand

something to cover your work surface: newspaper or an old plastic tablecloth

What to Do

1. Take a trip with your child to a nursery or garden center and select a variety of succulents. Look for thornless varieties! Some examples are aloe, jade plant, hen and chicks (sempervivum), living stone, and donkey-tail sedum. Your nursery may have other varieties available. Encourage your child to choose plants she likes.

2. At home, cover your work surface and gather your materials together.

3. Your child can cover the drainage hole of the large pot with the curved bit of plastic. This will keep the gravel and soil from washing out, but allow water to drain. Then ask her to put a layer of rocks or pebbles in the bottom of the pot.

4. Now she should add sandy soil to the pot and pat it smooth.

5. Help her to remove the plants from their nursery pots and plant them in the big pot. When all of the plants are in place, sprinkle the surface of the soil with sand.

6. Water the plants. Explain to your child that most succulents are desert plants. They store water in their thick, fleshy leaves. Water your succulents about once a week, and let them get fairly dry between waterings.

7. Find a warm, sunny location for your new garden.

8. As you create the garden, bits of the succulents will almost certainly break off. Do not worry! Save these pieces. In a week or two, they will send out tiny thread-like roots and you will be able to add them to your garden or start a new, small garden in another pot.

Propagate a Geranium

Start with one plant and make more! Geraniums are easy to grow and are appealing houseplants.

What You'll Need

a small bag of gravel (sold for fish tanks)

geranium plant (for a fragrant experience, choose a scented geranium)

potting soil

scissors

small cups, glasses, or jars of water

small flowerpots

some small pieces of curved plastic, cut from deli containers

What to Do

1. You and your child can talk about some different ways plants get started: for example, seeds, bulbs, and, surprisingly, from cuttings.
2. Show your child how to make a cutting from a geranium plant–then let her make several independently.
3. Place each cutting in a container of water. Wait and watch for the roots to form.
4. Once the roots look strong, help your child prepare the pots. Cover each drainage hole with a piece of curved plastic, then put a little gravel in the bottom of the pots on top of the plastic.
5. Fill each pot with potting soil, make a hole in the dirt with your finger, and settle the new plants gently into the holes.
6. Water them well, and give them a home on a sunny windowsill.
7. These little plants make great gifts. (See "Plant a Gift" on page 64.)

Another Thought

Try this with other plants. Coleus and impatiens are two garden plants that start easily from cuttings and can be grown in pots indoors.

27

Garden up a Salad

You can grow salad greens up in the air even if you have no garden area at all!
A window, porch, or balcony with a hanging basket will produce enough for
several meals.

What You'll Need

hanging planter basket

rocks or pebbles

seeds or bedding plants
suitable for salad (lettuce,
nasturtium, arugula,
or spinach)

soil

watering can

Books to Share

A Gardeners Alphabet
by Mary Azarian

The Vegetables We Eat
by Gail Gibbons

What to Do

1. Have your child place a layer of rocks or pebbles in the bottom of the planter. (This helps with drainage.)
2. Next, help her add soil to the planter, almost to the top. Water the soil so it is damp but not soaking.
3. Sprinkle with seeds. Scatter seeds so that the plants are not too crowded, then lightly cover the seeds with soil. Water again.
4. If you prefer to use bedding plants, help your child dig holes in the soil with her hands and settle the small plants in. Water them.
5. Hang the planter where it will get lots of light. Direct sunlight in the morning is good, but many salad plants do well in partial shade, especially in the afternoon.
6. Water when the soil feels dry.
7. Thin the seedlings as necessary as the plants grow. You can add these tiny plants to your salads. Otherwise, simply harvest, wash, and eat as the plants grow.

Garden in a Wading Pool

If you have a sunny spot outside, here is a way for you and your child to have an outdoor garden that involves no digging at all.

What You'll Need

several large bags of potting soil

small wading pool

trowel or small rake

vegetable and flower seeds of your choice

watering can

What to Do

1. Poke a dozen or so holes in the bottom of the wading pool so that it will not turn into a swamp when you water it. This is an adult step. Put it in a sunny spot where you want it to stay. When you are finished, it will be too heavy to move easily.

2. Your child will love helping you fill the pool with potting soil. Fill it to within 2" of the top. This is a great opportunity to play!

3. When you are through playing in the dirt, your child can rake it smooth and water it well. Let it sit overnight so the water can drain and the dirt can settle. The next day, add more dirt if necessary.

4. Now, you have a garden plot, ready to plant. You and your child can decide what you want to plant and what arrangement of plants will be pleasing.

5. Plant seeds or small plants, just as though you were planting in the ground. Water, wait, and watch: the three W's of gardening.

Another Thought

If you have no spot that gets sun all day, you can use this same idea by planting a child-sized garden in an old wheelbarrow. With your help, your child can move this garden around your yard or patio to keep it in the sun.

Chapter 3
Theme Gardens

Butterfly Garden

Everybody loves butterflies. You can encourage them by planting one or two flowers they like, or a whole garden full.

What You'll Need

plastic cups (poke a hole in the bottom for drainage) or small pots

soil

several of the following seeds or small plants: bee balm, butterfly bush (buddleia), foxglove, heliotrope, lupine, morning glory, nasturtium, Queen Anne's Lace, snapdragon, sweet William, viburnum, yarrow

sunny outdoor garden spot or planters

sunny windowsill

What to Do

1. Decide on a place for your butterfly garden. It will need plenty of sun: for butterflies to be active, they must have warmth and sunlight. You can use an established garden site, a window box, or hanging planters. Talk with your child about the design of the garden, choosing plants in different colors, scents, and heights.

2. If possible, include a bench or other seating and some bricks or rocks as part of the design. The rock or brick can be doused with sugar water occasionally to give the butterflies an extra treat.

3. If you are using seeds, plant them in the plastic cups. Put them on a sunny windowsill and keep the soil moist. When the seedlings are about 2" tall, transplant them to your garden or planters and remember to water them.

4. If you are using small plants, plant them directly in the ground and water well. Now, enjoy the flowers and wait for the butterflies to come!

5. For another butterfly treat, occasionally put out some juicy sliced fruit.

6. Just for fun, cut some butterfly shapes out of clean plastic milk cartons. Your child can decorate them with permanent markers and fasten them to slender sticks. These make charming garden decorations.

Another Thought

If you have room for a butterfly bush (buddleia), you will attract butterflies very quickly.

32

Busy Buzzing Bee Garden

Bees are essential to the health of our gardens and our entire planet. If we give them what they need, they will give back to us many times over.

What You'll Need

bee-friendly plants (include spring bloomers such as: bee plant, borage, sage, daisies, or marigolds; summer bloomers, such as basil, mint, oregano, rosemary, sage, thyme, or tomato; and autumn bloomers: rosemary, verbena, cosmos, or sunflowers)

prepared garden bed

shovel or trowel

What to Do

1. This is a project that will benefit from a trip to the library. Before you begin, go to the library with your child and learn as much as you can about bees and what they do for us.
2. After the library trip, you and your child will be full of ideas, and you can decide together what plants you want to include.
3. Go to a plant nursery together to select the plants and seeds you need.
4. Now, plant your bee-friendly garden. You are going to make sure the bees have food to eat from spring to fall.
5. Work with your child to arrange the garden with the tall plants at the back. Be sure to arrange them so that spring, summer, and autumn bloomers are intermixed.
6. Help your child plant everything and then water the garden bed.
7. If you can, add a misting sprinkler. Bees need moisture as well as food.

Another Thought

Do not mulch this garden. Some bees lay their eggs in the ground and cannot dig through mulch. Also, see "Bamboo Bee Abode" on page 56.

Grow Your Initials

Daisies for David, Marigolds for Marissa, Iris for Ivan, Petunias for Pablo. Creating a simple, special connection like this for your child can begin a life-long relationship with the natural world.

What You'll Need

prepared garden soil

seeds or plants with names that start with your child's initial

shovel or trowel

water

A Book to Share

A Gardener's Alphabet by Mary Azarian

What to Do

1. Do some research with your child to find out what vegetables, herbs, or flowers have names that start with the first initial of his name. Plan to plant one or more of these in your garden, or create a small garden of just these special plants.

2. Perhaps your child's name is reminiscent of an actual flower or herb, such as Lily, Rosemary, or Basil. You could include that plant in the garden. Or look into the Latin names or other common names of plants for inspiration. Lemon balm is melissa officinalis. Asters are also called Michaelmas daisies.

3. Gather the seeds and plants you have decided to plant, and you and your child can create this garden together. (See "Let's Make a Garden!" page 10.)

4. You could expand this idea in several ways. Plant a small garden in the shape of the initial, or plant your child's entire name: Daisy, Aster, Violet, Iris, Daffodil, for example.

Hummingbird Garden

It will take a little time for the hummingbirds to find your garden, but the wait is well worth it. They are unique tiny birds, endlessly fascinating to watch.

What You'll Need

a sunny garden plot or a sunny window box

appropriate flowers to attract hummingbirds in your area

shovel, trowel, other gardening tools as needed

water

A Book to Share

The Hummingbird Garden by Christine Baker Widman

What to Do

1. Look at some books about hummingbirds. See below for a suggestion.
2. Select the area where you want the hummingbird garden. You and your child should make this decision together. The location should be sunny and easy to see. It can be large or small; it can be a window box; it can even be a single plant.
3. Take your child to visit a local garden shop to learn which plants grow well in your area and will attract hummingbirds. Hummingbirds love red, and they are especially attracted to tubular flowers. Talking about this ahead of time will help your child pick out appropriate plants.
4. With your child, plant the flowers in the area you selected.
5. Water, wait, and watch. Be patient—it can take a while for the birds to find their way to a new garden.
6. If you hang a hummingbird feeder in your garden area, the birds may find you more quickly.

All-White Garden

An all-white garden produces an unusual and dramatic effect.

What You'll Need

adult-sized garden tools

child-sized shovel, spade, and hoe

fertilizer if needed

topsoil or compost (see page 48)

trowel

water hose

white and cream-colored flowering plants (some possibilities are white petunias, chrysanthemums, roses, white impatiens, and daisies) any other plants you choose that fit with the theme (white eggplant? snow-on-the-mountain? Be as creative as you want.)

What to Do

1. First, select the place for your white garden. Decide how big it will be and prepare the soil. (See "Let's Make a Garden!" on page 10.) As always for flowers and vegetables, you will need a sunny spot with easy access to water.

2. Next, visit a local nursery with your child. Talk with an employee about white or cream-colored plants that grow well in your part of the country. Encourage your child to ask questions and be sure that he helps pick out the plants.

3. Plant your garden, water it, and tend it. Enjoy the restful effect of the white flowers in midsummer.

Another Thought

This garden idea can be adapted easily to any color of your choice. If your child's favorite color is purple, you and he can plant a special garden full of purple flowers, purple vegetables (eggplant, some heirloom tomatoes), and purple herbs (purple basil). Let your child's imagination guide you.

Flower Shop Garden

With some pre-planning, you can create a delightful variation on the classic summer lemonade stand. This is a great project for a group of neighborhood children.

What You'll Need

a 4' x 4' area (mixed sun and shade)

blunt scissors

box cutter (adult use only, if you are using the cardboard box)

flowering plants (see "What to Do" for suggestions)

large cardboard box or a beach umbrella (optional)

markers

plastic vases or clear plastic cups

ribbon

shovel

small narrow folding table

small outdoor stool or chair

trowel

What to Do

1. In preparation, you and your child will have planted and tended a flower garden (see "Let's Make a Garden!" on page 10) with a variety of flowers. Some possibilities include asters, bachelor's button, phlox, cosmos, petunias, marigolds, and salvias.

2. When the flowers are ready for cutting, it is time to set up the flower stand. Be sure to talk in advance about how the children will use the money they earn and what they will do with any flowers that are left over at the end of the day. (Donating them to a local nursing home is one possibility.)

3. If you have a large cardboard box, such as an appliance box, you can cut a large opening in the front and a "door" in the back of the box. Your child can use the markers to decorate the box with flowers and leaves. This will provide shelter for the flower sellers and some shade for the flowers. If you do not have a big box, a beach umbrella is an effective and colorful alternative.

4. Set up a small table and a chair or two inside the box or under the umbrella.

5. Put the plastic vases and pre-cut lengths of ribbon on the table.

6. Use the blunt scissors to snip some blooms and take them into the flower shop.

7. Tie the blooms up with the ribbon, put them in the vases, and open your flower stand for business.

8. At the end of the day, be sure to follow up with the ideas you discussed for using the money and the extra flowers.

37

Memory Garden

This garden grows one plant at a time, and it is all about love and generosity.

What You'll Need

a prepared garden area
(see "Let's Make a Garden!"
on page 10)
_____

materials to make plant tags
_____

seeds and plants from friends
and relatives
_____

trowel or shovel
_____

water
_____

weather-proof permanent
marker or pen
_____

What to Do

1. The memory garden is a place to plant seeds and plants given by friends and family, or plants that have other special memories attached to them. When we see the plants growing or the flowers blooming, we can think of the people who gave us this enjoyment and remember the time we spent with them.

2. As friends and relatives give you plants and seeds, help your child plant them and mark each spot with a tag. This tag should have the name of the person who gave the seeds or plant and the name of the plant. Simple plant tags can be made from any weather-proof material. Be sure you print with a permanent marker or ink pen so the information does not wash away in the rain.

3. As you tend the garden together and the plants bloom and grow, talk with your child about how they remind you of people you love: the red zinnias from Nana who loves to wear red or the scent of Mr. Bauer's lemon balm tea.

4. You can add to the garden in other ways, too: maybe with special rocks from places you have visited or a brick from the wall that was removed when Auntie Gloria built her ramp. In this way, a memory garden can tell a very personal story of love and connection.

5. As the memory garden grows and blooms over the years, help your child continue the tradition by collecting seeds or dividing plants to share with others in turn.

Moon Garden

A garden blooming at night is sheer magic. Some flowering plants bloom at dusk and fade in the daylight, and some flowers release their fragrance only at night. Use all your senses to enjoy this garden.

What You'll Need

bedding plants of various night blooming varieties (see "What to Do")

a prepared garden plot (see "Let's Make a Garden! on page 10)

shovel, trowel, hoe

water

What to Do

1. Do some research with your child about plants that bloom at night. A good book to consult is *The Evening Garden: Flowers and Fragrance from Dusk till Dawn* by Peter Loewer. Night-blooming plants provide food for moths and other night-flying insects. The taller plants give shelter to fireflies.

2. Take a trip to a local nursery and choose a variety of night-blooming plants such as yucca, moonflower, evening primrose, four o'clocks, Angel's trumpet, night phlox, night-scented stock, fragrant columbine, flowering tobacco, August hosta, and citron daylily. One very familiar flower that releases its fragrance at night is the petunia.

3. Now, you and your child can arrange the plants in the flower bed. Put yucca and the other tall plants in the center of a bed so that you can approach from all sides, or in the back of a bed that is against a wall or fence.

4. Help your child plant everything and water it well.

5. Plan some special times to be outside at night to observe your Moon Garden. Be sure to include the night of the full moon!

Sensory Garden

We think of gardening as nourishment for our eyes and our sense of smell, but we do not always think of the other senses when we are planning a garden.

What You'll Need

a large garden plot (6' x 6')

a variety of plants (see "What to Do")

card stock

clear contact paper

garden stakes

shovel or trowel

What to Do

1. You and your child should prepare your garden area, as described in "Let's Make a Garden!" on page 10.

2. Plant some of the following plants in groups to represent the five senses.
   Touch: Lambs Ear (silky), Silver Sage (wooly), and Teasel (spiny). These plants will create an area where your child can touch and experience various textures.
   Taste: Nasturiums, peas, Swiss chard, and all of the mints are safe plants for a child to taste and explore.
   Smell: Honeysuckle, Lavender, Roses, peppermint, thyme, sage, chamomile, and Lemon Balm all have wonderful scents.
   Sight: Giant sunflowers, Poppies, Zinnias, Marigolds, Purple Sage, and Verbena have brilliant colors to create a dazzling visual display.
   Hearing: Rattlesnake Grass, Bamboo, and Love-in-a-Mist all produce distinctive sounds when brushed up against or as they move in the wind.

3. Use stones or other natural materials to create a path that will guide visitors on a walk through the sensory garden. If you have the space, add a little bench or garden chair at the end of the walk where you can rest and contemplate your journey.

4. Using card stock, create an identifying sign for each sensory area. Your child can make the signs using crayons or markers. Cover the paper on both sides with clear contact paper and post the signs on garden stakes.

5. Encourage your child to guide visitors through the garden and demonstrate how to explore it with their five senses.

Another Thought

Add birdfeeders and listen for birds singing. Notice the smell of wet grass and the fragrance of the dirt after you have watered the garden.

Invite These Plants to Tea

A tea party is a whole different experience if you actually grow the "tea."

What You'll Need

plants of peppermint, spearmint, monarda (bee balm), anise hyssop, catnip, or lemon balm

---

shovel or trowel

---

water

What to Do

1 Introduce your child to the wonderful taste sensations of herbal teas gathered right from the garden. Plant tea herbs such as anise hyssop (delicate licorice flavor), catnip (slightly minty taste), lemon balm (like lemon drop candy), and monarda or bee balm (also called Oswego tea, reminiscent of Earl Grey tea). There are also several intriguing flavors of mint: peppermint, spearmint, pineapple mint, apple mint, and even chocolate mint. All these plants grow easily and require very little attention.

2 Be aware that many herbs spread rapidly by underground roots or reseed freely. To keep them in line, either plant them at the edge of your garden where it will be easier to thin them out without disturbing the other plants, or help your child plant them in pots and keep them on the patio. Use no pesticides or herbicides. You may want to plant them close to your back door or keep the pots on your back steps. That way, they will always be handy for nipping off a few leaves for a quick cup of tea.

3 Show your child how to strip a few leaves off a selected plant, put them in a cup, and watch as you pour boiling water over them. Let your child place a saucer over the cup as it steeps for a few minutes. Swirl in a bit of honey or sip it plain. Delicious!

4 To keep your iced herb teas from getting diluted, make ice cubes from the tea. Teach your child how to pour cooled herb tea brew into ice cube trays.

Herb Garden for Cooking

If your child tends a few herbs in a small garden near your kitchen door, you will be creating a simple and satisfying connection between the garden and the food we eat.

What You'll Need

a sunny spot outdoors, easily accessible

a variety of herb plants, such as oregano, thyme, basil, parsley, mint, and lemon balm

What to Do

1. Go with your child to a nursery or garden center and select a variety of small herb plants.

2. Encourage her to rub the leaves of each plant very gently. Encourage her to describe each fragrance and think about what it reminds her of. She will probably identify the mint with toothpaste or gum, the oregano with pizza, and the lemon balm with lemonade.

3. Help her transplant the plants into a sunny corner of your yard. Most herbs require minimal care and will grow in almost any sunny location. Many of them grow back year after year, and the more you pick, the more they grow!

4. For cooking, you can use herbs either fresh or dried. Ask your child to pick some oregano, some parsley, and some basil the next time you are making spaghetti sauce. Add a sprig of mint to a glass of lemonade. Growing herbs offers a satisfying entry point into understanding where our food comes from.

Grow Your Own Pizza

A pizza garden or a garden pizza—either way, you and your child will love this idea.

What You'll Need

a garden plot in full sun, about 4' by 4'

gardening tools

stake and string

two small plants of each of the following: onions, tomatoes, mild peppers, parsley, oregano, and sweet basil

A Book to Share

Grow Your Own Pizza: Gardening Plans and Recipes for Kids by Constance Hardesty

What to Do

1. Prepare the garden plot, as described in "Let's Make a Garden!" on page 10. Add compost to enrich the soil. (As you read through the directions below, you will see that you could "Grow Your Own Pizza" in the wading pool of "Garden in a Wading Pool," on page 29.)
2. Tie a 2' length of string to a stake, and tie a smaller stick to the other end.
3. Put the stake in the center of the plot and show your child how to drag the smaller stick all the way around to mark out a circle, 4' in diameter.
4. Divide the circular plot into six equal wedges, one for each ingredient.
5. Help your child plant the ingredients in the different "slices."
6. Now, you and your child can tend the plants and eventually harvest them.
7. Use your home-grown pizza ingredients with crust and cheese to produce a truly home-grown pizza.

Chapter 4
Taking Care of Your Garden

Garden Markers

To keep track of what is growing, children design and construct garden row markers from painters' stir sticks and cardboard as well as protective plastic covers. Each row will be labeled with a custom-designed picture and name to identify what is growing.

What You'll Need

one of each of the following for each row:

cardboard squares, 2 per marker, cut to fit inside the baggies, painters' wooden stir sticks, zip-top pint-sized baggies

―――――――

glue

―――――――

permanent markers

―――――――

stapler

―――――――

What to Do

Your child can do every step, with supervision and help as needed.

1. Count out one wooden painters' stir stick for each garden row that you wish to label. Next, count out two cardboard squares and one zip-top baggie for each stick. Spread these out on the workspace.

2. One cardboard square will be the front and one will be the back. On the front cardboard square, draw a picture of the vegetable you wish to label. Is it carrots, tomatoes, beans, or okra? Draw that vegetable with permanent markers. You may also write the name of the plant in bold letters. If you wish, do the same for the other cardboard square that will be the back of the label, but this is not required.

3. Place the back label (design side down if any) on the workspace. Squirt a thick line of glue in the center of the cardboard from the top to the bottom. Lay the wooden stick on the glue. Draw another line of glue on the stick, and place the decorated cardboard (design side up) on the stick. The stick is now sandwiched between the two pieces of cardboard. Let the glue dry, and continue making as many labels as you need. Let all of them dry overnight.

4. Slip the cardboard end of the label into the zip-top baggie. Close the zipper right up to both sides of the stick. Staple the zipper closed so it will not come unzipped. Do this for all the labels.

5. If you wish, use permanent markers to draw designs on the sticks, too.

6. Take all the completed markers to the garden and push the sticks firmly into the soil at the end of each garden row.

Weeding

Weeding is an important part of the gardening routine. If you work alongside your child, you will find it just as much fun as planting and watering. Your attitude is the key.

What You'll Need

bucket

gardening gloves (optional)

trowel

What to Do

1. Take a garden tour with your child, observing and talking about the different plants and pointing out the differences between the garden plants and the weeds. Explain that weeds are just plants growing in the wrong place! They are valuable for supplying birds and insects with food and shelter, but they take water, sunlight, and nutrients from the garden plants, so they have to be removed from the garden.

2. After the tour, it is time for some practice. Have your child shadow you the first few times and continue to help him distinguish the weeds from the garden plants. This can be difficult when the plants are just coming up, but it gets much easier as the plants mature.

3. Toss the weeds into a bucket as you work. When you are finished, your child should put them into the compost (see page 48), as they have good nutrients to give back to the soil. Be sure, however, that you are not putting seed heads in the compost, or they will continue to grow (like weeds!). This is one reason to weed often. If you pull the weeds when they are small, they do not have a chance to produce seeds.

Another Thought

It takes attention and practice to tell weeds from seedlings. Give your child lots of encouragement and support, and make this whole activity an enjoyable challenge. It is a good job for the morning, when everyone is fresh and the earth is cool and moist.

Making Compost (the Traditional Way)

This may sound a little technical at first, but do not allow yourself to be daunted. Read all the way through. The process is simple and the results are truly "black gold" for the garden.

What You'll Need

black plastic

enough dry and wet herbicide-free materials to start a compost pile (see "What to Do")

pitchfork

stones

water

A simple alternative:

By far the easiest way to compost is to let it make itself. You can bury your kitchen scraps (no meat or dairy) at least a foot deep in an unused part of your garden. Do this daily or weekly in side-by-side sections, and by next year, that part of the garden will be fertile and ready to plant.

What to Do

1. Select an appropriate sunny spot for your compost pile, close to your garden. If you want to hide it from view, buy or build a screen–lattice, this is an easy material to use for this.

2. Start with a layer of dry materials such as dry leaves. Let your child play in them first to break up large pieces. On top of this, place a layer of fresh horse or cow manure if you can get it easily (farms and riding stables may give this to you free), then a layer of dirt. Keep alternating layers of dry and wet ingredients (sawdust, fresh grass clippings, straw, kitchen scraps (do not use any meat or dairy scraps), leaves and stems of weeds, crushed eggshells, used stable bedding) until your pile is about 4' high. It will shrink down as it "cooks."

3. Your child can collect and add materials. She can be in charge of scraping food scraps into a container to take out to the compost pile at the end of every day.

4. Water the whole pile as your child holds onto the hose or watering can with you.

5. Cover the pile with black plastic, weighted down with a few heavy stones, to start the cooking action.

6. When steam rises from your pile, it is ready to turn. Using a pitchfork, turn the pile upside down, mixing it well. As your child watches or holds onto the pitchfork handle with you, point out the heat and the white patches that show the compost is working to become soil that will feed the garden.

7. Water the pile again if it seems dry, and replace the covering. Turn the pile every week, and soon you will have an earthy-smelling, nutrient-dense compost.

Roly Poly Composter

Here is a high-energy way to approach the idea of making compost.

What You'll Need

a ½" wood bit

a few bricks

brown materials, such as leaves, sticks, shredded newspaper, cardboard

bungee cord

drill

green materials, such as fruit and vegetable scraps, grass clippings, used coffee grounds, egg shells

plastic trash can, with lid

safety glasses

Books to Share

Composting: Nature's Recyclers
by Robin Koontz

Compost Stew
by Mary McKenna Siddals

What to Do

1. Drill holes all over the sides and bottom of a plastic trash can (your child may be able to do this with assistance from you).
2. Place equal amounts of green and brown material inside the can. Green materials include fruit and vegetable scraps, grass clippings, used coffee grounds, and egg shells. Brown materials include leaves, sticks, shredded newspaper, and cardboard.
3. Add a small amount of water to the can (enough to make the materials moist but not soggy).
4. Then, put the lid on top and secure it with a bungee cord.
5. Lay the can on its side, and ask your child to roll it around the yard several times to mix everything up. She will love this step!
6. Once everything is well mixed, set the can on top of a few bricks (to allow air to move underneath the can), and your composter is ready for action.
7. Keep adding compostable materials, keep them damp, and give your child the job of rolling the composter around the yard every few days (good luck trying to stop her!), and you'll have loads of rich soil to add to your garden.

Compost Tea Parties

For a surprising change, serve tea *to* your garden.

What You'll Need

bucket of water

cheesecloth or other loosely woven cloth

child-size teapot, old teakettle, watering can, or squeeze bottle

home-grown compost (your own or from a friend)

string

What to Do

1. Look at "Making Compost (the Traditional Way)" and "Roly Poly Composter" on pages 48 and 49. If you have your own compost to use, this activity will be even more satisfying.

2. Get a chunk of compost, big enough to fill your child's two cupped hands. Put the compost on a piece of cheesecloth (or any other loosely woven cloth, like an old-fashioned diaper). You will be making a giant compost teabag.

3. Gather up the cloth and tie it tightly with strong string.

4. Suspend the compost tea bag by the string in a bucket of water so it is near the bottom but not resting on it.

5. After about a week, the compost tea should be well brewed. Take out the teabag and decant the tea into a teapot or an old teakettle.

6. Your child can now serve cups of compost tea to the plants and flowers.

7. If your child isn't into tea sets, a small squeeze bottle or a watering can does the job just as well.

8. Be sure that anything used for compost tea is well washed afterwards, preferably in a dishwasher.

Homemade Worm Farm

Worms move and mix dirt. Their burrows make the soil looser, allowing air and water in to nourish the plant roots. Creating a worm farm allows you and your child to see some of this in action.

What You'll Need

a large round and clear container like the one a bakery cake comes in, with its platter

a medium or small round container that will fit inside the large one

a metal skewer or a Philips screwdriver

black construction paper

dry oatmeal

garden soil

sand

shovel

small container with a spray lid

tape

trowel

water

worms (about 25)

What to Do

Your child can be involved in all of these steps, working with you.

1. Find a place in your yard where you can dig up some rich dirt without disturbing anything.

2. Visit a bait shop and purchase some worms. If you don't want to purchase worms, you can dig for them in your yard. You will need about 25 worms.

3. Use a skewer or screwdriver to poke some air holes in the cake platter. This will be the lid for your worm farm.

4. Put the small round container in the large round container and center it.

5. Carefully fill the doughnut-shaped area between the two containers with a 1" layer of moist soil. Hold the center container in place so no dirt gets under it. Sprinkle a teaspoon of dry oatmeal on the soil, then add a ½" layer of moist sand. Continue in this way to about 2" from the top, with the last layer being soil.

6. Add the worms. Handle them gently. Don't try to push them under the soil. They'll go on their own in just a little while. Gently mist the entire area with water.

7. Put the lid (the cake platter with holes) on top of the worm farm. Press down to create a seal, but be cautious and don't harm the worms.

8. Tape black construction paper around the worm farm so it will be nice and dark. Put your worm farm in a cool, shady place. Keep it cool and keep the soil moist but not wet.

9. Every few days, remove the paper and observe how the worms are mixing the soil and the sand together. Add a small sprinkle of oatmeal every week.

10. You can keep your worm farm for two to three weeks, and then you should release the worms into your garden.

Make a Toad House

Invite toads into your garden for natural pest control. Toads eat insects, slugs, and snails—as many as 10,000 in a single summer!

What You'll Need

acrylic paints

paintbrush

saucer of water

shovel

small clay flowerpot

Books to Share

Frogs and Toads and Tadpoles, Too by Allan Fowler

Toad by the Road: A Year in the Life of These Amazing Amphibians by Joanne Ryder

What to Do

1. In preparation, talk with your child about how toads like to eat many of the insects, slugs, and snails that damage the flowers and foods in your garden. (See the suggested books.) You may be able to point out some examples of insect damage.

2. Discuss ways you might attract toads to your garden. Making them welcome by providing a special house is one way to do this.

3. Set out the flowerpot and the paints. Invite your child to decorate the flowerpot in any way he wants.

4. Once the pot is dry, find a shady spot in your yard and dig a hole large enough for the pot to fit into on its side.

5. Place the pot in the hole and bury the bottom half (toads like to burrow into the moist ground).

6. Collect a few leaves from around the yard and place them inside the pot to create a cozy bed for the toad.

7. Add a small saucer of water nearby for your toad to sip from, and your toad house is move-in ready.

8. You could create a whole village of toad houses!

Backyard Bug Hunt

This is an observing and information-gathering activity. You and your child will explore your environment together and develop an increased appreciation for the life that surrounds us.

What You'll Need

insect books (field guides, picture books, as appropriate to your child)

jars with holes in the lids

magnifying glass

A Book to Share

Insects: Revised and Updated
by Herbert S. Zim and
Clarence Cottam

What to Do

1. First, you will want to visit the library with your child and check out as many books about insects and bugs as you can find. In addition, you may decide to buy a simple field guide to insects.

2. Look at the books together and talk about insects and bugs. Some are helpful to our gardens and some are not. Right now, we are just identifying them.

3. Now, head out into the yard with your collecting jars and your curiosity. Your whole purpose here is to observe and to learn about the insects that share your environment.

4. Encourage your child to search attentively and collect the bugs she finds, carefully putting them into the jars. Be sure she understands that all living creatures need air to survive, which is why the collecting jars need holes in the top.

5. Once collected, examine the insects with your child. Use a magnifying glass to take a closer look at the insects. Help her describe each one with attention to details: this will help you find the ones you do not recognize in the field guide.

6. Release the insects back into their habitat. The more you and your child learn about the creatures that live here with us on the earth, the richer your shared experience in the garden will be.

Handpicking as Natural Pest Control

Some insects and bugs are harmful to our gardens, and we need to remove them for the garden to thrive.

What You'll Need

container

liquid dish soap

tweezers (optional)

water

What to Do

1. Building on the "Backyard Bug Hunt" (page 53), do some research on the harmful bugs you want to target so that you and your child can properly identify them.

2. Put a few drops of liquid dish soap in an empty container, such as a yogurt or cottage cheese container. Add water to make a soapy solution.

3. Talk about removing harmful bugs from the garden so the flowers and vegetables can thrive.

4. Show your child the container of soapy water. Explain that the soap makes the surface of the water slippery so the bugs will drown quickly.

5. Go out to the garden with your child and check the plants for bugs that are eating the leaves. Some bugs that are easy to handpick are slugs, Japanese beetles, and Colorado potato bugs. It's even easier in the early morning when the pests move more slowly.

6. One at a time, pick or tap the bugs off and drop them into the soapy water. Be sure there are no leaves floating in the water; otherwise, the bugs may climb on them and fly away to chew on the garden leaves later.

7. If you notice many bugs chewing leaves on one particular type of plant, show your child how to check underneath the leaves for tiny eggs. More bugs will hatch from these eggs and go right to work destroying more leaves. You can pick the leaf with the eggs attached and stomp on it, or rub the eggs off with your thumb.

8. When you are finished, carefully dump out the soapy container of dead bugs and let your child stomp on them to be sure the pests are dead.

Another Thought

Your state or county may have a cooperative extension service. Someone there will be happy to help you identify leaf-munching bugs and may even have literature and pictures of target pests.

Planting a Natural Mosquito Repellent

**What a surprise! Lemon balm smells wonderful to us,
but mosquitoes fly the other way.**

What You'll Need

plant of lemon balm

shovel or trowel

water

What to Do

1. Choose a spot for the lemon balm to grow. Like many herbs, lemon balm can become invasive. It spreads by underground roots and will reseed as well. Give it a corner of the garden or yard where it can spread happily without pushing aside or shading other plants.

2. Help your child plant the lemon balm and demonstrate how to rub a leaf between your fingers to release the scent.

3. Explain that mosquitoes don't like the smell of this plant. Crushing a few leaves of lemon balm and rubbing the juice on your skin will keep most mosquitoes from biting for about an hour.

4. If your lemon balm plant is small, you may want to wait until it is well established before showing your child how to use the leaves as mosquito repellent. Most children will seek out the plant on their own, once they experience how effective it is. It should only take about a month for your lemon balm plant to establish itself and be able to handle the stress of having some leaves torn off.

5. Lemon balm also makes delicious tea that helps get rid of tension headaches and eases occasional insomnia. Crush a few leaves in a cup, add boiling water, and cover the cup with a saucer to keep in the steam and the oil from the leaves. After a few minutes, strain out the leaves (or leave them in for extra flavor), swirl in a spoonful of honey, and sip.

Bamboo Bee Abode

Create a home for the peaceful, native, non-stinging bees called "mason bees." These bees are slightly smaller than honeybees, and each one visits up to 1,000 blooms every day, **making them incredible pollinators.**

What You'll Need

1 or 2 bamboo canes about ¼" diameter (use fresh ones, if you have a stand of bamboo in your yard, or use the ones sold as plant stakes in garden centers, or see below for alternatives)

brown paper

markers or crayons

plastic sleeve (this can be the bag your newspaper arrives in, or a page protector)

saw

scissors

tape

twine

A Book to Share

The Bee Tree
by Patricia Polacco

What to Do

1. First, you need to cut the bamboo canes into 6" to 8" lengths. You will need about 12 pieces. (Adult step only).
2. Now, you or your child should cut a piece of paper that will fit inside the plastic sleeve, and your child can decorate it with crayons or markers.
3. Bundle the bamboo canes together, and tie them securely with the twine.
4. Put the decorated paper inside the plastic sleeve, press out the excess air, and tape the end closed.
5. Wrap this "bee wrapper" around the bundle, and fasten it securely. The plastic wrapper will protect the bees from rain.
6. Hang your Bee Abode horizontally in a warm, sunny spot near your garden. The female bees will fill the tubes with their eggs, nectar, and pollen to feed the young bees.

Another Thought

If you do not have bamboo, you can make a Bee Abode from paper drinking straws (plastic ones will not work). Use a bit of playdough to plug one end of each straw, and proceed as above. Another possibility is to use a block of seasoned wood. Drill holes in it with a long ¼" drill bit. Hang it so the round bee "doorways" are on the side.

Buzzz... Buzzz....

Harvesting and Sharing the Crop

Make harvesting your crop into an event. Everyone who has helped in the garden should be included in the celebration of the harvest.

What You'll Need

containers, both small and large

garden hose

gardening tools as needed (possibly clippers and trowels)

What to Do

1. This activity needs very little description. As your garden begins to produce, you and your child (and any other garden helpers) will have the pleasure of gathering in the harvest. Go out in the morning to pick what you need for the day; or go out right before mealtime to gather salad greens, peas, or herbs for the meal.

2. Use containers that are easy for little hands to hold and carry.

3. Use the garden hose or a large bucket of water to wash the produce before you bring it indoors. This washing can be as much fun for the children as the picking itself!

4. Often, you will have more of a certain vegetable than you can use. This is an opportunity for generosity. Talk with your child about people who might need food. Do you have a neighbor who finds it hard to get out and shop? Do you have a food pantry or soup kitchen nearby? Take advantage of these precious opportunities.

5. Another way for you and your child to share your garden produce is by cooking together. Consider gifts of homemade tomato sauce, zucchini bread, or carrot cake. You will think of many other possibilities.

Chapter 5
Just for Fun

Seed Packet Puzzles

Simple puzzles use seed packets and any extra seeds.

What You'll Need

4" × 6" index cards

a variety of seed packages

child-safe scissors

white glue

What to Do

Your child can do all of these steps, with supervision.

1. Remove the seeds from one of the packages and glue a few seeds onto one end of an index card.

2. Glue the cover of the seed package to the other end of the index card.

3. Repeat for each type of seed and seed package.

4. After the glue is dry, cut the seed end and the picture end of each card apart in a distinctive pattern to create a set of simple two-piece jig-saw puzzles that will help you and your child learn to recognize seeds.

5. For an even simpler variation, save your seed packets and glue the pictures to index cards. When the glue is dry, cut each of the cards into two or three pieces. Now you have simple picture-matching puzzles.

My Own Beanstalk

Bring a very familiar story to life.

What You'll Need

a small handful of gravel

a small piece of curved plastic, cut from a deli container

a small pot for planting (3"–6" in diameter)

a thin garden stake cut 12"–15" long

clear contact paper

crayons or markers

green bean seeds

index cards, or heavy paper cut into squares

potting soil

tape

the story of "Jack and the Beanstalk"

What to Do

1. Read or tell your child the story of "Jack and the Beanstalk." Shake a few bean seeds out of the packet and talk about planting your own "magic seeds."

2. Give your child a small pot. Help her cover the drainage hole with the small piece of curved plastic, then put a handful of gravel on the bottom of the pot. This will keep the soil from washing out when you water the beanstalk but will also allow for drainage.

3. Ask her to fill her pot ¾ full with potting soil. Now she can use her fingers to make three small holes, place one seed in each hole, and cover them with more soil. Water thoroughly.

4. On one index card, your child can draw a picture of Jack, and on another card, a picture of the castle. Cut them out, if you want.

5. Cover the front and back of the cards with clear contact paper.

6. Help your child tape her picture of Jack about 4" from the bottom of the stake and tape the picture of the castle to the top.

7. Put the garden stake into the pot.

8. Keep the soil moist but not soaking wet. As the vines grow, wrap them around the garden stake to encourage them to climb.

All Five Senses in the Garden

Every now and then, it is good to stop and pay close attention. Think like an animal, with sharp ears and a keen sense of smell. What would it be like to be a dog in the garden? What would you notice? Suppose you were a tiny spider? What would you see?

What You'll Need

a garden

What to Do

1. Have some conversations with your child about how we notice things and learn things using all five of our senses, not just one or two.

2. Create an outing to a garden. This can be your own garden, a community garden, a rose garden in a park, an arboretum, a commercial pick-your-own orchard or garden, or even a garden center.

3. When you arrive, both of you should stand very still and look around you very carefully. After about a minute, encourage your child to describe what he sees, using color words and descriptive vocabulary. Tell him what you noticed, too. Make this a conversation.

4. Once again, stand very still—but this time be very, very quiet. Concentrate on listening. After about a minute, talk about what you heard. You may want to repeat this once more, as quiet listening is sometimes hard for us the first time.

5. Invite your child gently to touch the leaves, flowers, and fruit and describe the various textures, such as smooth, rough, prickly, fuzzy, or sticky.

6. Now, encourage your child to smell the flowers and plants and describe which ones are sweet, sour, or funny-smelling. What else can you smell in the garden? Do you notice the smell of wet dirt? Newly mown grass? We sometimes forget about our sense of smell as a way to learn about our environment.

7. If appropriate, invite your child to pick a fruit or vegetable, supervising closely. After he washes and tastes his food, talk about the taste. Is it sweet? Sour? A little of both? Is there any other way to describe the flavor?

My Green-Haired Friends

This gives you and your child a chance to watch grass grow and to have some laughter and storytelling fun in the process.

What You'll Need

craft sticks or tongue depressors

easy-growing grass seed (rye is a good choice)

markers

newspaper, if you are working indoors

paper or foam cups (for extra fun, use cups of varying sizes)

potting soil

water

watering can or small pitcher

A Book to Share

Hubert's Hair Raising Adventure by Bill Peet

What to Do

1. This is a good outdoor activity. If you do it indoors, cover the work area with newspaper.
2. Give your child a few paper or foam cups. Poke two or three holes in the bottom of each one with a pencil. Now, he can use the markers to draw faces on the cups. If you have cups of different sizes, this could be a green-haired family!
3. Put an extra cup next to the potting soil to use as a scoop. Your child should fill each cup with dirt to about ½" from the top.
4. Show him how to sprinkle grass seed onto the soil.
5. Cover the seeds lightly by sprinkling soil on top of them with your fingers.
6. Water the cups with a slow stream of water from a watering can to dampen the soil.
7. Ask your child if he wants to name his cup characters. If he does, you can use the craft sticks to label them with their names.
8. Put the cups in a sunny spot, keep them damp, and check the progress of the seeds daily.
9. Pretty soon, your green-haired friends will need fancy haircuts.

Plant a Gift

Plants make welcome gifts, for any occasion or for no occasion at all. Decorating a special pot adds a loving, personal touch to the gift.

What You'll Need

a few handfuls of gravel (easy to buy in plant shops and with aquarium supplies)

acrylic paints

clay flowerpots, about 4" across, and saucers to fit

clear resin spray (found at hobby stores)

flower seeds or small flowering plants

moist potting soil

newspaper

small paintbrushes

small pieces of curved plastic, cut from deli containers

water, for washing brushes and watering the plants

What to Do

1 Set up your workspace, covering the surfaces with newspaper to protect them.

2 Set out the clay flowerpots and saucers and the painting supplies.

3 Have your child place her pots upside down on the newspaper and paint designs on them. (It's nice to write the date on the bottom.)

4 Leave the pots on the newspaper and allow them to dry thoroughly.

5 When the paint is dry, spray them generously with clear resin spray (adult-only step). Let them dry overnight.

6 When they are completely dry (not even tacky), help your child cover the drainage hole with a piece of curved plastic and add a small handful of gravel to the bottom of the pot. This will keep the soil from washing out but also allow for good drainage. Fill the pots with potting soil to within ½" of the top, and place the saucers under each pot.

7 Help your child, as needed, to plant either the seeds or small flowers and water thoroughly. (You might look at "Propagate a Geranium," on page 27, and "Memory Garden," on page 38.)

8 Place the pots in a warm, sunny window until they are ready to give as gifts.

Spider Web Sweet Peas

The garden pea patch will resemble a fairy glen with fragrant sweet peas climbing through a spider web of twine. Before planting sweet peas (or snap peas), weave heavy twine between two garden poles in a spider web design. The web will be a base for the climbing vines.

What You'll Need

2 bamboo poles, about 6' tall

a sunny garden area, at least 4' wide

heavy twine

scissors or garden shears

spade or shovel, trowel

sweet pea seeds (or snap pea seeds or small plants)

water, sun, and time to grow

What to Do

1. You will need to help your child prepare the bamboo poles and begin making the twine spider web. To do this, lay the two poles flat on the grass, about 3' apart. Tie them together in two places, first at the tops of the poles, and then about a foot from the bottoms. (Leave about 1' of pole clear at the bottom so the poles can be pushed into the garden soil.)

2. Next, make an X with twine: tie a long piece from the top left corner to the bottom right corner, and then repeat tying twine from the top right to the bottom left, crossing over in the middle. Tie the twine in the middle with a bow or knot.

3. With long pieces of heavy twine, begin tying twine strands to form a web look. It does not have to be perfect in spacing or design—a random web design is more magical and spider-like.

4. When the web is complete, you and your child, working together, can stand the two poles upright and carry them carefully to the garden area where the peas will be planted. Push each pole into the garden soil a little at a time until both poles are about 6" to a foot deep in the dirt and standing strong. The web will be spread between the two poles.

5. Plant sweet pea seeds or snap pea seeds as directed on the package, or dig holes and plant small plants. Plant along the base of the web between the poles. Water, sunshine, and waiting! The pea vines will twine their way through the web, working their way into the weaving and creating a magical web of flowers and greenery.

Miniature Garden

This is an idea with special appeal to children who like to create stories with small figures and animals. It is all about imagination and fun. Building a living, outdoor setting for play can be endlessly absorbing.

What You'll Need

rocks, sticks, moss, sand, wood chips (as desired)

shade-loving plants

shallow plastic bowl

small, shady garden spot (about 3' x 3')

toy figures and animals

trowel, old spoons, old forks (anything that can be used as a miniature tool)

What to Do

Your child's imagination is the guide here. There are no rules.

1. Find the perfect spot for your miniature garden. Mark the edges with a small wall made of rocks or sticks.

2. Make paths and roads through your garden with small rocks, sand, and wood chips, or simply smooth the dirt with your hands and rake it with a fork.

3. Build some miniature log cabins by stacking sticks together. Cover the roofs with moss. Use a little white glue, if needed.

4. Add some shade-loving plants such as impatiens, coleus, and violas.

5. Dig a small hole and put a shallow plastic bowl into it. Fill the bowl with water for a pond.

6. Enjoy imaginary play in your miniature garden using the toy animals and figurines.

Garden Stone Arrangements

Collect and save stones of all sizes to make unique arrangements throughout the garden. Create pathways, borders, or simply add color, design, and shape anywhere at all.

What You'll Need

garden

old towel

rake

rocks, stones, gravel, pebbles

scrub brush

trowel or spade

tub or bucket for water

What to Do

Your child can be involved at every stage of this open-ended activity.

1. Collect and save rocks of all kinds. A river or beach is a great place to find rocks, stones, and pebbles. Digging in the garden will reveal rocks of all sizes. Whenever you see a rock you like, pick it up and save it. It may take a while to collect enough rocks for your garden, but however many you have, there will be something you can do with them that makes the garden more beautiful.

2. Get the rocks ready. Put them in a tub of water and scrub with a brush until clean. Dry them in the sun, or pat them dry with an old towel. Spread the rocks out on an old towel, tarp, or on the grass to see what you have.

3. Now, look at the garden with the eye of an artist and start to make plans. Think about what you can do with the rocks you have collected. Decide what you like best and begin!

4. Some ideas for decorating the garden with rocks:

   Tower Stack: Stack three or more rocks in a tower. Begin with a large flat rock, and then place a slightly smaller rock on top of the first, a smaller rock on top of the second, then a third, and so on. Try to balance the rocks to make a tower.

   Border: Line the garden with rocks to create a border that defines the edges. Borders may also be made around individual plants to make sections in the garden. A border can also define a pathway.

   Stone Path: Small stones, pebbles, and gravel can form a small pathway in the garden when placed by hand, or a larger pathway when poured from a bucket or shoveled from the wheelbarrow.

   Art Stones: Find an area of the garden that is bare, and place stones in any design you wish. A spiral, circle or "pie" shape can make a garden look more interesting. Fill in with smaller pebbles, gravel, or sand to give color and texture.

Bean Pole Teepee

The garden bean patch will become a secluded space for your child and her friends to read and dream. Before planting beans, weave the bean poles with ribbons, yarn, twine, and string. After the beans grow tall, spread a quilt inside the greenery, crawl in, read, and imagine.

What You'll Need

a sunny garden area at least 5' in diameter

bean seeds or small bean plants

collection of weaving materials, such as yarn, twine, ribbons, surveyor's plastic, string, or torn strips of fabric

heavy twine

old blanket or quilt

scissors or garden shears

spade or shovel, trowel

step ladder

tall bean poles (four to eight of them); these can be wooden garden poles, bamboo poles, or other choices; 12' long poles work well

What to Do

1. An adult should prepare the bean poles in the garden. Push each pole deep into the garden soil, arranging them in a teepee fashion. Keep an open space in the center about 5' in diameter. Where the poles meet at the top, wrap and tie them together securely with heavy twine. Your child can help as appropriate.

2. Now, your child and her friends can start wrapping strands of twine from one pole to the next. Be sure to leave a space for the doorway opening.

3. Keep adding and wrapping weaving strands of all kinds, filling the areas between the poles. Encourage your child to work as high up as she can reach easily. Later, the bean vines will take care of the rest of the undecorated area.

4. At the base of each pole, plant bean seeds as directed on the package, or dig holes and plant small bean plants.

5. Water, sunshine, and waiting! Bean vines will grow day by day, twining their way up the poles and working their way into the children's weaving.

6. When the vines have reached the top of the teepee, it is time to celebrate! Place an old quilt or blanket inside the teepee. Bring books and a small picnic, if you wish. Children can crawl inside the bean pole teepee to enjoy the green space.
   A bean pole teepee is a restful place for an afternoon nap. Nibbling on green beans fresh from the vine is allowed!

Index

Index

Index